Smash.
autumn 2004

Published 2004

**Editorial and new arrangements and engraving by
Artemis Music Limited (www.artemismusic.com)
Cover Design by Space DPS**

3 AM

words and music by

**Charlie Simpson, James Bourne, Mathew Sargeant,
Lauren Christy, Scott Spock and Graham Edwards**

highest chart position 1
release date 26th July 2004
did you know Busted's Charlie Simpson is also in a thrash metal
band called Fightstar

It's o - kay, _____ but that _____ was yes - ter - day _____ and now _____ I'm
that we _____ are more _____ than meant _____ to be? And now _____ you're

driv - ing in my car, _____ words won't get me far, _____
driv - ing in your car, _____ but you won't get far, _____

(3° see block lyric)

____ when they told me. _____ Oh. _____
____ 'cause your car is _____ Oh. _____

I'm call-ing you at three A. M. _____ and I'm _____ stand-ing here _____ right out - side your door,

(Lyrics on D.S.)
Driving in my car
Words don't get me far
When they tell me
Oh.

I'm calling...

Babycakes

words and music by
Liana Caruana, Marc Portelli and Nicholas Gallante

highest chart position 1
release date 9th August 2004
did you know 3 Of A Kind were first heard on a pirate radio station in their native Hackney

Ba - by cakes, you just don't know, know, how I, I, how I like it down

low, low. And I just want you to know that I think our love will grow. Gon-na

take it step by step be - cause I'm not some - thing you own.

Rap 1 (Male):

Confused don't know what I'm feeling
Confused relationships without meaning
In the mist I can see it gleaming
Time to wake up and stop the dreaming
'Cause your my lil' Baby cakes
And I know you got what it takes
The way you make me feel
The way that I am
When you talk to you friends
And you call me your man
Tell her I gotta thank you, thank you,
Feel good the better, the future's just me and you
With our fun time, whether fun's loaded,
There's just one thing I want you to know

Rap 2 (Female):

Lovin' every minute
Just you and me
And I'm still dreaming
You'd be my baby
Maybe there's a possibility
We grow old together live happily
And you're great
It's a song for everyone
At the first sight you know it's love
Sexual tension physical attractions
Instant flip flirtatious actions

Burn

words and music by

Bryan Cox, Jermaine Dupri and Usher Raymond

highest chart position 1
release date 28th June 2004
did you know Usher's ambition when he was a kid was to own a Krispy Crème cookie factory

burn for me___ to say this,   but it's com - ing from___ my heart.___   It's been a
(Verses 2 & 3 see block lyrics)

long time___ com - ing,   but we'd have been fell___ a - part.___   I real - ly

want to work___ this out   but I don't think you're gon - na change___ and   I

do but you don't___ think it's best we   go our sep - 'rate ways.___

To Coda ⊕

Verse 2:
Sending pages I ain't supposed to
Got somebody here but I want you.
'Cause the feeling ain't the same
Find myself calling her your name.
Ladies tell me do you understand?
Now all my fellas do you feel my pain?
It's the way I feel
I know I made a mistake, now it's too late
I know she ain't coming back
What I gotta do now to get my shoulder back
Ooh ooh ooh
Man I don't know what I'm gonna do
Without my boo hoo.
You've been gone for too long
It's been fifty-leven days, um-teen hours
I'll be burning till you return.

Verse 3:
I'm twisted 'cause one side of me is
Telling me that I need to move on
On the other side I wanna break down and cry
Ooh I'm twisted 'cause one side of me is
Telling me that I need to move on
On the other side I wanna break down and cry.

Hoo...

Cannonball

words and music by
Damien Rice

highest chart position 19
release date 5th July 2004

did you know Damien's album 'O' was originally released, without much UK success, in 2001. Since the success of the re-recorded version of 'Cannonball' it has become a platinum seller

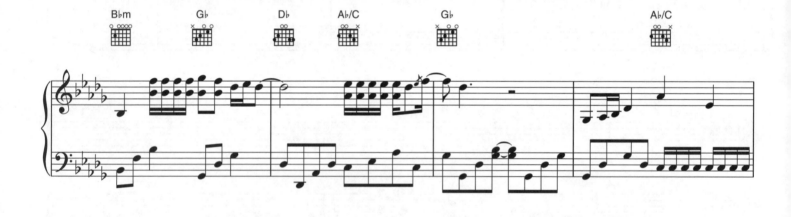

There's still a lit-tle bit of your taste____ in my mouth,____ still a lit-tle bit of you__ laced
There's still a lit-tle bit of your ghost,____ your wit - ness. There's still a lit-tle bit of your face

(Verse 3 see block lyric)

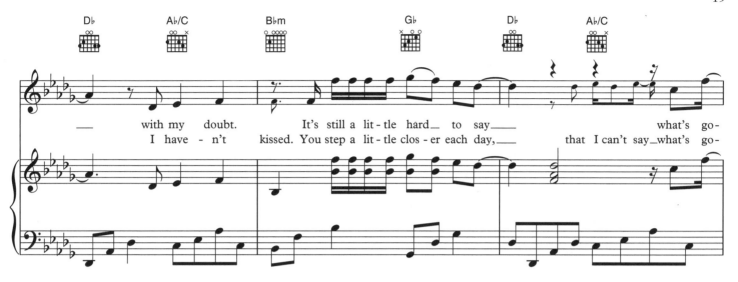

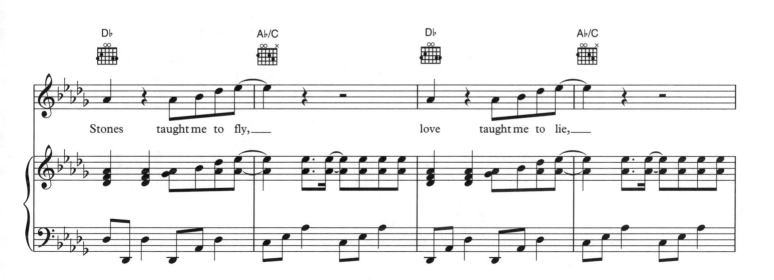

Verse 3:
There's still a little bit of your song in my ear
There's still a little bit of your words I long to hear
You step a little closer to me
So close that I can't see what's going on.

Forca

words and music by
Nelly Furtado, Gerald Eaton and Brian West

highest chart position 40
release date 12th July 2004
did you know 'Forca' was the official song of the Euro 2004 football tournament in Portugal. Nelly, whose parents are Portuguese, says the lyrics are about "the love of the game"

It is the pas - sion flow-ing right__ on through your veins,__
It is a sound - track of your ev - er flow - ing life,__

and it's the feel - ing like you're oh__ so glad you came.
it is the wind__ be - neath your feet__ that makes you fly.__

Caught In A Moment

highest chart position 8
release date 23rd August 2004

did you know When former Atomic Kitten (before they were famous) singer Heidi Range auditioned for Sugababes, she wasn't told which band she was trying out for, and didn't find out until she'd passed the audition

words and music by

Jonathan Lipsey, Marius De Vries, Karen Poole, Keisha Buchanan, Mutya Buena and Heidi Range

Your stare swal-lows me___ and I can hard-ly breathe,___ I feel it's___ dan-ge-rous,
(Verse 2 see block lyric)

could be dead - ly.___ Some-how I'm will - ing___ to do the things you want,___

Verse 2:
Broke through barriers and passed the state of mind
I'm not scared no more, it feels divine.
So take me in and catch me when I fall
I'm waiting on the edge, uncut my soul.
Snip by snip
I'm losing it bit by bit
I'm taking it step by step
Boy here tonight.

For Lovers

highest chart position 7
release date 12th April 2004

did you know Pete Doherty officially supports the Thamkrabok
monastery in Thailand, where he went to get over his drug problems

words and music by
**Peter Doherty, Peter Wolfe, Julian Taylor,
Ned, Maff Scott, Matthew White, David Banks
and Jake Fior**

Lyrics:

I'm run-ning a-way_ with you,_ that's all I_ ev-er do._

That's all we ev - er mean,_ but I for-give_ you_ ev-r'y-thing.

Meet me at the rail-road_ bar_ a-bout
I've paid the pen - al-ty,_ you're the jailer

Pumps

words and music by
Amy Winehouse and Salaam Remi

highest chart position **did not chart**
release date **23rd August 2004**
did you know **According to Amy, Pumps is a dig at "girls who think they have to go out and meet an athlete, then their life will be perfect"**

I Don't Wanna Know

highest chart position 1
release date 31st May 2004

did you know As well as being a famous performer in his own right, Mario is one of the most sought-after producers in the business, and has worked with Whitney Houston, Mary J Blige, P Diddy, Jennifer Lopez and R Kelly

words and music by

Mario Winans, Michael Jones, Chauncey Hawkins, Erick Sermon, Parrish Smith, Ethne Brennan, Nicky Ryan and Roma Ryan

Rap:

I don't wanna know where your whereabouts or how you movin'
I know when you in the house or when you cruisin'
It's been proven, my love you abusin'
I can't understand, how a man got you choosin'
Undecided, I came and provided
My undivided, you came and denied it
Don't even try it, I know when you lyin'
Don't even do that, I know why you cryin'
I'm not applyin' no pressure, just wanna let you know

That I don't wanna let you go
And I don't wanna let you leave
Can't say I didn't let you breathe
Gave you extra cheese
Put you in the SUV
You wanted ice so I made you freeze
Made you hot like the West Indies
Now it's time you invest in me
Cause if not then it's best you leave.

Help Yourself

words and music by
**Amy Winehouse, Jimmy Hogarth,
Frederick James and Larry Stock**

highest chart position **did not chart**
release date **23rd August 2004**

did you know Since the release of her debut album 'Frank' Amy
has been nominated for two MOBO Awards, two Brit Awards, the
Mercury Music Prize and she won a prestigious Ivor Novello Award
for Best Contemporary Song

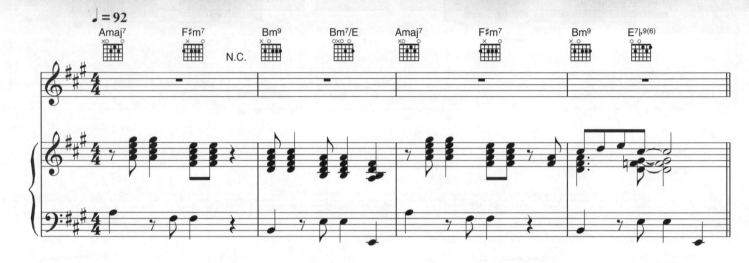

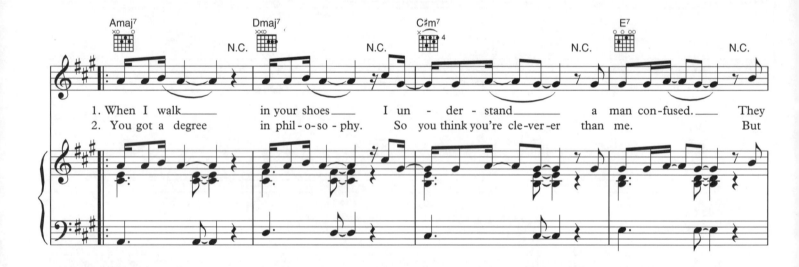

1. When I walk____ in your shoes____ I un‑der‑stand____ a man con‑fused.____ They
2. You got a degree in phil‑o‑so‑phy. So you think you're cle‑ver‑er than me. But

much too big,____ but I____ don't care____ I feel____ the weight____ your shoul‑ders bear.____
I'm not just____ some dra‑ma queen.____ 'Cause it's where you at____ not where you been.____

Laura

words and music by

Scott Hoffman and Jason Sellards

highest chart position 12
release date 7th June 2004
did you know Scissor Sister Jake Shears once paid for a holiday
by go-go dancing around the bars of New York

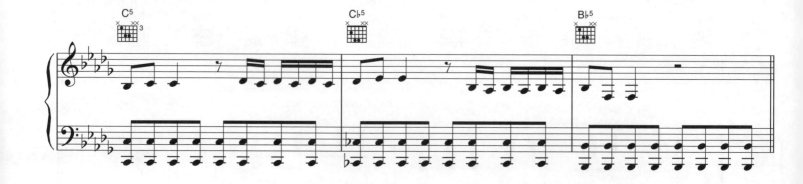

More More More

words and music by
Gregg Diamond

highest chart position **not released at time of printing**
release date **4th October 2004**
did you know 'More More More' was a 1970s disco classic and was performed in 1976 by adult movie star Andrea True. Look out for the homage in Rachel's video!

Ooh, _____ how do you like my love?

But if you want to know how I real - ly feel, _____

get the cam - 'ras rol - ling, get the ac - tion go - ing. Ba - by you know my

Love Machine

highest chart position 2
release date 13th September 2004

did you know In the *Pop Stars: The Rivals* battle for No 1, Girls Aloud claimed the top spot and outsold boy band One True Voice by a whopping 66,000 copies in the first week

words and music by

**Miranda Cooper, Brian Higgins, Timothy Powell,
Nick Coler, Lisa Cowling, Shawn Mahan
and Myra Boyle**

Lad-ies you're damn_ right, you can't read a man's_ mind, we're liv-ing in two_ tribes and

My Happy Ending

words and music by
Butch Walker and Avril Lavigne

highest chart position 5
release date 2nd August 2004
did you know Avril holds an unusual record – her song 'Complicated' had more radio airplay than any other song for an astonishing 11 weeks, beating Madonna's record by a week

68

Never Felt Like This Before

words and music by
Richard Nowels and Shaznay Lewis

highest chart position 8
release date 4th July 2004

did you know As well as singing, Shaznay was the main songwriter in All Saints, writing, among others, 'Never Ever' and 'Pure Shores'

The Show

words and music by

**Miranda Cooper, Brian Higgins, Timothy Powell,
Lisa Cowling and Jonathan Shave**

highest chart position 2
release date 28th June 2004

did you know Having scored a huge hit with a cover of East 17's
'Stay Another Day', the girls hope to claim the Christmas No.1 with
another cover version, this time Frankie Goes To Hollywood's
'The Power Of Love'

If it's not you, oh no, I won't do that. You'll have to wait for me and that is that.

Obviously

words and music by
James Bourne, Thomas Fletcher and Danny Jones

highest chart position 1
release date 21st June 2004

did you know The name 'McFly' comes from the character Marty McFly in 80s teen movie *Back To The Future*, which is Tom from the band's favourite film

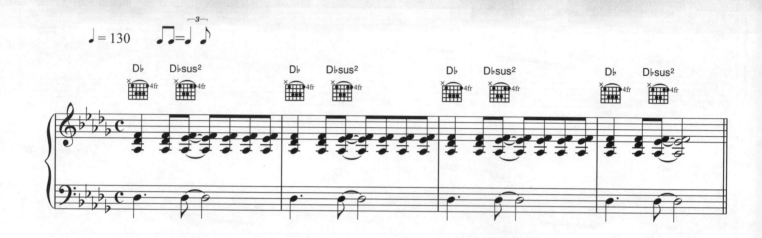

Re - cent - ly I've___ been_____ hope - less - ly reach - ing___

out for this girl___ who's out of this world, be - lieve me.___

she's out of my league.___ I'm wast-ing my time___ 'cause she'll nev-er be

mine and I know I nev-er will be good e-nough for her.___ No no.___

I nev-er will be good e-nough for her.___

Redneck Woman

words and music by
John Rich and Gretchen Wilson

highest chart position 42
release date 23rd August 2004
did you know Gretchen's favourite records are Patsy Cline's 'Greatest Hits', 'Back In Black' by AC/DC and 'The Essential Charlie Daniels'

Fast country ♩ = 94

N.C.

1. Well, I ain't

Verse:

nev - er   been the Bar - bie - doll   type.___   No,

2. *See additional lyrics*

I can't swig__ that sweet cham-pagne. I'd rath-er drink beer all night in a tav-

ern, or in a hon-ky-tonk, or on a four-wheel-drive tail - gate.__

I've got post - ers on__ my wall__ of Sky-nyrd, Kid and Strait. Some

peo - ple look__ down on__ me, but I don't give a rip.__ I

Verse 2:
Victoria's Secret,
Well, their stuff's real nice.
Oh, but I can buy the same damn thing
On a Wal-Mart shelf, half price
And still look sexy,
Just as sexy as those models on TV.
No, I don't need no designer tag
To make my man want me.
You might think I'm trashy,
A little too hard-core,
But in my neck of the woods,
I'm just the girl next door.
(To Chorus:)

Sick And Tired

highest chart position 4
release date 2nd August 2004
did you know Anastacia describes the sound of 'Sick And Tired'
as 'sprock' – a fusion of soul, pop and rock

words and music by

**Dallas Austin, Anastacia Newkirk
and Glen Ballard**

My love is on the line,

my love is on the line. My love is on the line, my love is on the line. (De

My love is on the line, my love is on the line.
la li a bib bot a wah de la de. De la li a bib bot a wah de la de.)

Single

words and music by
**Natasha Bedingfield, Andrew Frampton,
Stephen Alan Kipner and Wayne Wilkins**

highest chart position 3
release date 11th May 2004
did you know Natasha carries a dictaphone with her everywhere,
in case she thinks up some lyrics while on the move

Some Girls

words and music by
Richard Phillips and Hannah Robinson

highest chart position 2
release date 12th July 2004
did you know The title of Rachel's album 'Funky Dory' is a tribute to David Bowie's 'Hunky Dory', and the title track contains a homage to a song from that album, 'Andy Warhol'

My ba - by drives a car.___ (Hey!)
Foot - loose and fan - cy free.___ (Woah.)___

He calls me when he wants.___ (Hey!)
My ba - by waits for me.___ (Woah.___ Oh.)___

Spectacular

words and music by
Graham Coxon

highest chart position 32
release date 26th July 2004

did you know Former Blur guitarist Coxon owns his own record
label called Transcopic which he uses to release his own records
and others by a string of unusual artists, including American
maverick Billy Childish

some-thing quite spec-tac - u - lar.

Guitar solo

I'd

112

Story Of My Life

words and music by
**Kristian Leontiou, Peter Wilkinson
and Sarah Erasmus**

highest chart position 9
release date 24th May 2004
did you know Before hitting the charts, Kristian worked as a hairdresser in north west London

1. You say it was like this, I was torn be-tween two worlds.
2. See I was just think-ing, now my life is on the road.

One full of pro-mise and the truth I knew would hurt.
The straight and the nar-row, on the route that I've been shown.

That Girl

words and music by
James Bourne and Thomas Fletcher

highest chart position 3
release date 6th September 2004
did you know 'That Girl' was the first McFly song ever written, and was penned by Tom from the band along with James from Busted when they were writing tracks for Busted's second album

One two three four!

Went out with the guys and be - fore
We spoke for hou - rs, took off my

(Verse 3 instrumental)

my eyes there was this girl, she looked so fine.
trou - sers, spent the day laugh - ing in the sun.

And she blew my mind,_____ and I wished that she___ was mine,_____
And we___ had fun,_____ and my friends they all___looked stunned._____

and I___ said: "Hey wait up 'cause I'm off to speak to her."_____
"Dude she's a - maz - ing and I can't be - lieve you got that girl."_____

*("Nev - er get her, you're nev - er gon - na get that girl,_
("She's a - maz - ing, I can't be - lieve you got that girl,_

And my friends said:_____ But I did - n't care_
And my friends said:_____ It gave me more street cred,_

* Backing vocals written
octave higher than sung.

lone - li - ness has been a friend of mine._____ And my friends said:_

*("Such a pi - ty, I can't be - lieve you lost that girl,___ it's such a pi - ty, I

I let her slip___ a - way,___ they

* Backing vocals written
octave higher than sung.

can't be - lieve you lost that girl,___ it's such a pi - ty, I can't be - lieve you lost that girl.)

tell me ev - 'ry day_____ it will be___ o - kay.__

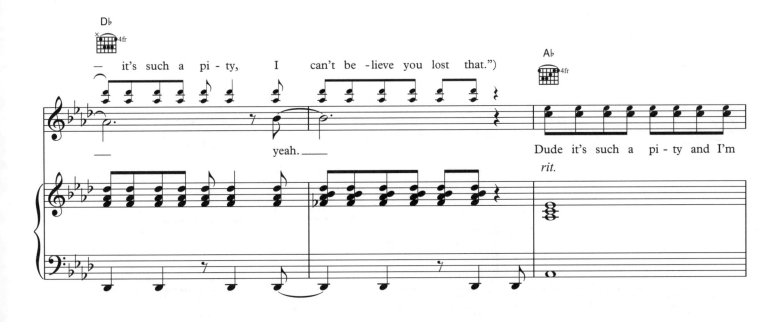

Strict Machine

words and music by
Alison Goldfrapp, William Gregory and Nick Batt

highest chart position 20
release date 12th May 2004
did you know Alison Goldfrapp got her first break singing backing vocals on Orbital's 'Snivilisation' album. They discovered her yodelling while milking a cow at a party!

Super Duper Love
(Are You Diggin' On Me?) Part 1

words and music by
Willie Garner

highest chart position 18
release date 10th May 2004
did you know Joss was first noticed after winning TV talent show *Star For A Night* at the age of just 14

Medium funk

Yeah,

are you dig - gin' on me? _____ Yeah, _____

132

These Words

highest chart position 1
release date 16th August 2004

did you know 'These Words' became the first song to top the official UK charts and then top the official UK download charts the following week – it outsold the No.2 song by more than two to one

words and music by

Stephen Alan Kipner, Andrew Frampton, Natasha Bedingfield and Wayne Wilkins

Verse 2:
Read some Byron, Shelley and Keats
Recited it over a hip-hop beat.
I'm having trouble saying what I mean
With dead poets and drum machines
You know I had some studio time booked
But I couldn't find a killer hook
Now you're gonna raise the bar right up
Nothing I write is ever good enough.

We Are

words and music by

Andreas Carlsson and Jorgen Elofsson

highest chart position 8
release date 2nd August 2004

did you know Ana co-wrote 'We Are' with fellow Swede Max Martin, who has written songs for Justin Timberlake and Britney Spears

Wishing On A Star

words and music by
Billie Calvin

highest chart position 11
release date **30th August 2004**

did you know 'Wishing On A Star', taken from Weller's album of cover versions, was originally a No.3 hit for disco band Rose Royce in January 1978

Trick Me

words and music by
Dallas Austin

highest chart position **2**
release date **24th May 2004**

did you know **In one of the unlikeliest pairings in pop, there is a version of Bjork's song 'Oceania' circulating on the Internet which features guest vocals by Kelis**